WHAT CHRISTIANS
Have *Always*
BELIEVED

'The author, Timothy Cross, is intent on making disciples. After we are born again of the Spirit of God, indwelt by the Holy Spirit, we are to grow up into the fullness of Christ.

This book, full of biblical truth, will assist with the growing up aspect of our Christian lives. Good theology, plainly presented, is essential for the disciple of Jesus. Here is a tool for both those new in the faith and for those who want to go deeper into the essentials.

Thank you for this helpful book, Timothy Cross, a brother in Christ.'

—Kent Philpott, Pastor

Miller Avenue Baptist Church

Mill Valley, California USA

'What Christians believe changed sunset to sunrise in the ancient world and the whole course of human history. Followers of Jesus went out to turn everything upside down and announce a new beginning for the whole world. Christianity gave rise to great civilisations, architecture, music, poetry, and art as people all across the world were swept up into the life of the Living God, Father, Son and Holy Spirit. In this delightful, fresh and punchy book, experienced writer and theologian, Timothy Cross, sets out with compelling clarity and incisive ability the central doctrines of the Christian Faith. An excellent resource for old and new alike to immerse ourselves in and having done so go out with a new song to sing, a flag to follow and a story to tell, that may once more change the world.'

—Revd Marcus Nelson

Vicar St Marks Evangelical Anglican Church

Cardiff, Wales

WHAT CHRISTIANS
Have *Always*
BELIEVED

Essentials of the Christian Faith

TIMOTHY CROSS,
BA (Hons), BD (Hons), Th.D., Litt.D

AMBASSADOR INTERNATIONAL
GREENVILLE, SOUTH CAROLINA & BELFAST, NORTHERN IRELAND

www.ambassador-international.com

What Christians Have Always Believed

Essentials of the Christian Faith
©2021 by Timothy Cross, BA (Hons), BD (Hons), Th.D., Litt.D
All rights reserved

ISBN: 978-1-64960-029-5
eISBN: 978-1-62020-745-1

Cover Design and Page Layout by Hannah Nichols
eBook Conversion by Anna Riebe Raats
Edited by Daphne Self

AMBASSADOR INTERNATIONAL
Emerald House
411 University Ridge, Suite B14
Greenville, SC 29601, USA
www.ambassador-international.com

AMBASSADOR BOOKS
The Mount
2 Woodstock Link
Belfast, BT6 8DD, Northern Ireland, UK
www.ambassadormedia.co.uk

The colophon is a trademark of Ambassador, a Christian publishing company.

The chapters of this book are based on the doctrinal framework of the Leckwith Gospel Hall, Cardiff, entitled 'Our Beliefs.' Sincere thanks to the Elders — notably Mr. Keith Hamber — for granting me permission to use these as the basis for this work.

CONTENTS

INTRODUCTION

The pages that follow seek to explain and unfold some of the essential doctrines of the Christian Faith — what all Christians believe and are required to believe. Ministering in various churches as I am privileged to do, I am sometimes surprised when even professed Christians of longstanding seem to be somewhat hazy on foundational Christian truths. This book is my humble attempt to rectify the matter. Firm foundations are vital if a building is not to collapse. Likewise, if we are to remain stable in these tumultuous days, how important it is to be firmly grounded and founded on the truth of God as revealed in His Word. I commend this work to the triune God, praying that He would be pleased to use it for the salvation of souls, the edification of His people and the glory of His Name.

—Timothy Cross

Cardiff

Wales

UK

CHAPTER ONE

CHRISTIANS BELIEVE IN THE DIVINE INSPIRATION, AUTHORITY, AND SUFFICIENCY OF THE HOLY SCRIPTURES

'Of making many books there is no end . . . ' said 'the Preacher' in Ecclesiastes 12:12 (RSV). If that was so in his day, it is surely even more so today, with the advent of e-books and advances in printing technology making books easier and quicker to produce.

THE BOOK OF BOOKS

Of all the millions of books in the world, however, there is one Book which stands out on its own, in a category all its own. That Book is the Bible — also known as the Holy Scriptures. Why is this so? It is so because throughout the ages Christians have believed and have proved — and continue to believe and prove to this day — that the Bible is no ordinary book but the very Word of God Himself: the Word of God written and preserved for our eternal blessing and benefit.

> *A glory gilds the sacred page*
> *Majestic, like the sun*
> *It gives a light to every age*
> *It gives, but borrows none.*
>
> (William Cowper 1731-1800)

We have just said that Christians believe that the Bible is the Word of God. To be more specific, we would have to say that Christians believe that the Bible is 'the divinely inspired Word of God.' The divine inspiration of the Holy Scriptures is one of the bedrock fundamentals of the Christian Faith. All else actually depends on, and flows from, this, for it is the divine inspiration of the Scriptures alone which accounts for their supernatural nature and ensures the absolute truth and authority of every one of its words and lines, making them a sure foundation for our earthly and eternal welfare. But, what exactly do we mean by the words 'divine inspiration?'

'THEOPNEUSTOS'

In 2 Timothy 3:16 we read 'All Scripture is inspired by God and profitable for teaching, for reproof, for correction, and for training in righteousness.' The word 'inspired' here means 'God breathed.' It is the word 'theopneustos.' It refers to the ministry and influence of the Holy Spirit of God, working in the hearts, minds, mouths, and pens of the human authors of the Bible, ensuring that they wrote exactly what God wanted and intended us to know. The Spirit of God ensured that fallible men wrote infallibly the very words of Almighty God. Divine inspiration ensured that men subject to error — as we are all subject to error — produced inerrant writings, writing free from error. 'Because no prophecy ever came by the impulse of man, but men moved by the Holy Spirit spoke from God' (2 Peter 1:21).

Divine inspiration therefore — the working of the Holy Spirit of God in and through the various human authors of Scripture — is that which ensures the absolute truth of Scripture in all that it teaches and affirms: how the universe came into being; how the world is in the present state that it is; the way of salvation; how we should live our lives; the ultimate goal of the universe and much more. Remarkably, therefore, the Bible alone can be considered as 'The Maker's Manual' — a revelation of the one true God and His will and His ways.

THE DIVINE AUTHORITY OF THE HOLY SCRIPTURES

The divine authority of the Holy Scriptures is the logical and theological corollary of the divine inspiration of the Holy Scriptures. The ultimate authority is, of course, Almighty God Himself. Scripture is His Word. Scripture is thus to be believed and obeyed as God Himself is to be believed and obeyed. Woe betides anyone who does otherwise! We are therefore obliged to be beholden to Scripture, to submit ourselves to its authority for all that we believe and how we are to behave.

As the very Word of God, Scripture has its own intrinsic authority. 'And we also thank God constantly for this, that when you received the word of God which you heard from us, you accepted it not as the word of men but as what it really is, the word of God, which is at work in you believers' (1 Thessalonians 2:13).

In a nutshell: 'The authority of the Holy Scripture, for which it ought to be believed and obeyed, dependeth not upon the testimony of any man or Church, but wholly upon God (who is truth itself) the author thereof, and therefore it is to be received, because it is the Word of God' (*Westminster Confession of Faith,* Chapter IV).

THE DIVINE SUFFICIENCY OF THE HOLY SCRIPTURES

In 2 Timothy 3:15 we read that 'the sacred writings' (the Holy Scriptures) are able to instruct you for salvation through faith in Christ Jesus.' The Scriptures therefore were given to us by God primarily so that we could know the way of salvation — to know that all is eternally well with our souls — that our sins are forgiven and we have peace with God our maker, and will dwell in His glorious presence eternally, rather than be banished to the flames of hell. But how is salvation known and enjoyed? Says the verse, 'through faith in Christ Jesus.'

It is Christ who is the key to the Scriptures. The written word and the living Word are one. The incarnate Word is the key which unlocks the inspired Word. Scripture is given to point us to the Saviour and avail ourselves of the salvation He has procured for all who believe in Him. Herein then lies the incomparability of Scripture. No other book can reveal to us how we can be eternally saved.

Apart from Scripture, we would be stumbling in the dark and eternally lost. Thank God then for the Scriptures. Read them. Meditate on them. Believe them. Know them. Obey them. Seek the help of the Holy Spirit who wrote them to understand them. They are God's Word, and, uniquely among all books, reveal the secret of a happy life, a happy death, and a happy eternity. They are all-sufficient for this, and hence the warning on the last page of the Bible to neither add to them nor subtract from them: 'I warn every one who hears the words of the prophecy of this book: if any one adds to them, God will add to him the plagues described in this book, and if any one takes away from the words of this prophecy, God will take away his share in the tree of life and in the holy city, which are described in this book' (Revelation 22:18,19).

Interestingly, chapter VI of the *39 Articles of the Church of England* is entitled 'Of the sufficiency of Holy Scripture for salvation.'

It reads as following: 'Holy Scripture containeth all things necessary to salvation: so that whatsoever is not read therein, nor may be proved thereby, is not to be required of any man that it should be believed as an article of Faith, or be thought requisite or necessary to salvation. In the name of Holy Scripture, we do understand those Canonical books of the Old and New Testament, of whose authority were never any doubt in the Church.'

The Bible then is absolutely foundational, essential, and indispensable to the Christian Faith. Christians believe in its divine inspiration, submit to its divine authority, and rejoice in its all sufficiency and saving vitality. Truly, there is no book like the Bible!

> *How precious is that Book divine*
> *By inspiration given*
> *Bright as a lamp its doctrines shine*
> *To guide our souls to heaven.*
>
> *Its light, descending from above*
> *Our sin-sick world to cheer*
> *Displays a Saviour's boundless love*
> *And brings His glories near.*
>
> *It shows to man his wandering ways*
> *And where his feet have trod*
> *And brings to view the matchless grace*
> *Of our forgiving God.*
>
> *It lights our path, it lifts our hearts*
> *Along the upward way*
> *It life and joy and peace imparts*
> *Till dawns eternal day.*
>
> (John Fawcett 1739-1817)

QUESTIONS AND POINTS TO PONDER

1. A secular book may be described as 'inspiring.' But what do Christians mean when they assert that the Bible is 'inspired'?

2. All non-Christian religions either add to or detract from the Bible. List some of these and explain how they deviate from Scripture.

3. If the Bible really is God's Word, we ought to know it! Do you have a regular, daily time with God's Word? If not, what adjustments to your lifestyle could you make to ensure you do?

4. 'The Old and New Testaments are the two lips by which God speaks.'

CHAPTER TWO

CHRISTIANS BELIEVE IN THE UNITY OF THE GODHEAD WITH THE DISTINCTION OF THREE PERSONS IN THAT UNITY, NAMELY THE FATHER AND THE SON AND THE HOLY SPIRIT, TO WHOM EQUAL HONOUR IS DUE

Invariably, the final words uttered in a Christian gathering for public worship on the Lord's Day — the first day of the week — are these: 'The grace of the Lord Jesus Christ and the love of God and the fellowship of the Holy Spirit be with you all' (2 Corinthians 13:14). These words take us to one of the essential, non-negotiable doctrines of the Christian Faith, and a, if not *the,* touchstone of Christian orthodoxy. We refer to the doctrine of the Trinity.

THE HOLY TRINITY

The Christian Faith is a Trinitarian faith. Christians are characterised by the belief in the divine trinity — in a triune God — and Christians are characterised by the worship of this triune God. Why? Because the God who has revealed Himself in His Word, the Bible, has revealed Himself to be a triune God. In a nutshell, the one, true and living God has revealed Himself as Father, Son, and Holy Spirit. God is one and God is three. God is three and God is one. This, of course, is above and beyond human comprehension. So we say with Isaac Watts (1674-1748):

Almighty God to Thee

Be endless honours done

The undivided Three

And the Mysterious One

Where reason fails with all her powers

There faith prevails and love adores.

The *Shorter Catechism* delineates the strict monotheism of the Bible when it asks the question:

Are there more Gods than one?

And answers it:

There is but one only, the living and true God.

Yet the *Shorter Catechism* also delineates the revealed trinitarianism of the Bible, when it asks the question: 'How many persons are there in the Godhead?'

And answers it: 'There are three persons in the Godhead — the Father, the Son, and the Holy Ghost; and these three are One God, the same in substance, equal in power and glory.'

Lawson's comment here is helpful. He explains: 'The Bible tells us that the Father is God, the Son is God, and the Holy Spirit is God. And yet it tells us that these three persons form only *one* God, exist and act together as one, and must be honoured and worshipped alike. This is a subject on which we know nothing except what is revealed.'

THE TRINITARIANISM OF THE BIBLE

The divine trinity is actually implicit on the very first page of the Bible. The Bible begins with the affirmation 'In the beginning God created the heavens and the earth' (Genesis 1:1). The word for 'God' here is 'Elohim' and this is a plural word in Hebrew — compare one 'cherub' and more than one 'cherubim.' This suggests a plurality within the one God, and this is confirmed in the following verses where we have reference to 'the Spirit of God . . . moving over the face of the waters' (1:2) and the various references to the Word of God in the refrain 'And God said . . . ' (1:3 et al.). We know from the New Testament that this refers to the Lord Jesus Christ, as John 1:14 tells us that in Christ 'the Word became flesh and dwelt among us.'

It is in the New Testament however that the full-orbed doctrine of the divine trinity is revealed. We see this at the outset of the Saviour's public ministry — at His baptism in the river Jordan. When Jesus — 'the second person of the Trinity' — was baptised in the Jordan, the Bible records 'the Spirit of God descending like a dove, and alighting on him; and lo, a voice from heaven, saying, "This is my beloved Son, with whom I am well pleased" (Matthew 3:16,17). The voice in question being none less than the voice of God the Father.

The divine trinity is also revealed at the close of the Saviour's public ministry, as well as at its outset. The risen Saviour's 'Great Commission' to His disciples was a Trinitarian one. His command to them was and His current command to the Church still is to 'Go therefore and make disciples of all nations, baptizing them in the name **(not 'names')** of the Father and of the Son and of the Holy Spirit' (Matthew 28:19, author's emphasis).

ONE-NESS AND THREE-NESS

Christians believe that God is three and God is one. Scripture reveals that this is so. The basic creed of the Old Testament is that 'The LORD our God is one LORD' (Deuteronomy 6:4). This God — the God of creation and the God of the covenant — is the only true and living God. Hence, He tolerates no rivals. Hence the sin of idolatry — honouring false gods — is condemned so strongly in the Bible. God stipulates 'You shall have no other gods before me' (Exodus 20:3). He alone deserves, requires, and is worthy of our exclusive allegiance and obedience, solely because He alone can say 'I am the LORD, and there is no other, besides me there is no God' (Isaiah 45:5).

Yet Scripture also reveals three distinct Persons within the unity of this one God. God the Father is God — 'for us there is one God, the Father, from whom are all things and for whom we exist . . . ' (1 Corinthians 8:6). God the Son is God — Thomas confessed to the risen Christ 'My Lord and my God' (John 20:28) — the deity of Christ is part of the very fabric of the New Testament and the Holy Spirit is God. The Holy Spirit is both a Person and a divine Person.

The Bible teaches clearly that the Holy Spirit of God is a divine Person, rather than an influence or impersonal 'force.' First Corinthians 12:11 reveals that the Spirit of God gives gifts, and 'apportions to each one individually as he wills' — will, or volition being a characteristic of a person. Likewise, Ephesians 4:30 says 'do not grieve the Holy Spirit of God.' Again, only a person can be grieved. And the deity of this Person is evident from the unsavoury incident in Acts 5:3,4, where within two verses we read of a 'lie to the Holy Spirit' as being 'You have not lied to men but to God.'

Christians thus believe in the Trinity, because Scripture reveals that the God of the Bible is a Tri-unity. And Christians also believe in the Trinity because they have come into a personal experience of this triune God, for all three Persons of the Trinity have played a role in the believer's personal salvation. A Christian is one who has been made a beneficiary of the saving grace of the triune God:

TRINITARIAN SALVATION

In 1 Peter 1:2, Peter gives a full-orbed description of what it is to be a Christian, when he describes a Christian as 'chosen and destined by God the Father and sanctified by the Spirit for obedience to Jesus Christ and for sprinkling with His blood.' A Christian therefore is a Christian solely due to the work of the divine Trinity. We note a Christian as being:

'Chosen and destined by God the Father . . . ' The Bible stresses God the Father's eternal choice of us, rather than our choice of Christ in time,

'even as he chose us in him before the foundation of the world . . . '
(Ephesians 1:4).

Redeemed by Christ. Christ procured our salvation by His atoning death
at Calvary. 'He himself bore our sins in his body on the tree' (1 Peter 2:24). He
paid the penalty for our sins by shedding His precious blood. Faith unites us
to Him and makes the benefits of His redeeming work our own. This is what
Peter means by 'sprinkling with His blood.'

'Sanctified by the Spirit.' 'We are made partakers of the redemption purchased by Christ by the effectual application of it to us by His Holy Spirit'
states the *Shorter Catechism*, explaining our verse. Christ purchased our salvation, and the Holy Spirit puts us in actual possession of it, by convicting us
of our sin and need, drawing us to Christ and nurturing in us saving faith
in Him. Our Trinitarian salvation is thus a case of redemption both divinely
accomplished and divinely applied.

The Christian experience of salvation is therefore a triune experience. All
three members of the divine Trinity have cooperated and played a distinctive
role in our salvation. God the Father chose us and sent His Son to die for us.
God the Son purchased our salvation by His death and resurrection. God the
Holy Spirit has drawn us to Christ and through Him we are reconciled to God
the Father. Furthermore, our continued fellowship and experience of God is
also a triune one, for prayer — 'the Christian's native air and vital breath' is
made to God the Father, through the merits and mediation of Christ, in the
power of the Holy Spirit. 'Through him (Christ) we have access in one Spirit
to the Father' (Ephesians 2:18). 'God has sent the Spirit of his Son into our
hearts, crying, 'Abba! Father!'' (Galatians 4: 6).

So, Christians believe in the unity of the Godhead, with the distinction
of three Persons in that unity, namely the Father and the Son and the Holy
Spirit, to whom equal honour is due. The doctrine of the divine trinity is
central to the Christian Faith and Christian orthodoxy. It is a doctrine to
be believed as it is revealed in Scripture. It is more than a doctrine, however.

Underlying it there is a God to be known, a God to be trusted and adored, and a God to be worshipped:

Glory be to God the Father

Glory be to God the Son

Glory be to God the Spirit

Great Jehovah, Three in One

Glory, glory

While eternal ages run!

(Horatius Bonar 1808-1889)

QUESTIONS AND POINTS TO PONDER

1. The word 'Trinity' is not found in the Bible. Does this mean that the divine trinity is not biblical?

2. List some of the biblical evidences for the holy Trinity.

3. How would you set about explaining the Trinity to an interested but ignorant non-Christian friend?

4. 'All heresy is, in some way, a denial of the Trinity' (JC Ryle). In what way is this so?

5. Jehovah's Witnesses — along with other denials — deny the trinity and believe that the Holy Spirit is not a person but a 'force.' Why do orthodox Christians believe in the personality of the Holy Spirit?

6. 'If you wish to see the Trinity, go to the River Jordan' (Augustine). What did he mean by that?

CHAPTER THREE

CHRISTIANS BELIEVE THAT THE SON OF GOD TRULY BECAME MAN BEING BEGOTTEN OF THE HOLY GHOST AND BORN OF THE VIRGIN MARY

THE WONDER OF WONDERS

In 1 Timothy 3:16 the Apostle Paul exclaimed 'Great indeed, we confess, is the mystery of our religion: God was manifested in the flesh.' The Christian Faith is concerned primarily, not with a creed or a code of conduct — important though these are in their place — but rather with a particular Person: The Person of the Lord Jesus Christ. And the uniqueness of the Christian Faith stems from the uniqueness of this particular Person. But wherein lies the uniqueness of the Lord Jesus Christ? His uniqueness stems from His being the eternal Son of God, who, in a moment in time, took upon Himself a human body in the plan of God, and was born into our world to accomplish the salvation of His people. Scripture reveals that Christ is unique because He is the God-man — God in the flesh; the incarnate Son of God. 'For in him the whole fullness of deity dwells bodily' (Colossians 2:9).

But how did God, in Christ, become man? How was the bridge between heaven and earth, and between deity and humanity actually made? It was, the Bible says, by the Son of God's being conceived by the power of the Holy

Spirit and born of a virgin. Christ was conceived in the womb of a virgin who lived in northern Israel, a virgin by the name of Mary.

THE VIRGIN BIRTH OF CHRIST

The *Shorter Catechism* asks the question: 'How did Christ, being the Son of God, become man?'

The answer it gives summarises the teaching of Scripture when it states: 'Christ, the Son of God, became man, by taking to Himself a true body and a reasonable soul, being conceived by the power of the Holy Ghost, in the womb of the Virgin Mary, and born of her, yet without sin' (Q. 22).

Christians celebrate this fact every time Christmas comes around:

Though true God of true God

Light of Light eternal

The womb of a virgin He hath not abhorred

Son of the Father

Begotten not created

O come let us adore Him, Christ the Lord!

(Latin, 17th century, *Our Own Hymn Book*)

Christians believe in the virgin birth — or more accurately, the 'virgin conception' — of the Lord Jesus Christ. They do so because His virgin birth is plainly and emphatically taught in the Bible, the Word of God. Some 700 years BC, God foretold through the prophet Isaiah 'Behold, a *virgin* shall conceive and bear a son, and shall call His name Imman'u-el **(God is with us)**' (Isaiah 7:14, author's emphasis). In the fullness of time, God kept His promise, and the prophecy was fulfilled when 'the angel Gabriel was sent from God to a city of Galilee named Nazareth, to a virgin betrothed to a man whose name was Joseph . . . and the virgin's name was Mary' (Luke 1:26,27). To Mary's astonishment, Gabriel announced to her that she was to conceive a child via a miraculous conception, via the action of the Holy Spirit of God Himself.

THE SCRIPTURAL EVIDENCE

Matthew's Gospel records that 'Mary . . . was found to be with child of the Holy Spirit' (Matthew 1:18). Mary's pregnancy, understandably, caused acute consternation to Joseph, her husband to be. He feared the worst. He thought — logically and naturally — that Mary had been unfaithful, and so he sought to dissolve the impending marriage. He changed his mind and course radically however after receiving the following angelic assurance. An 'angel of the Lord' assured and reassured him 'Joseph, son of David, do not fear to take Mary your wife, for that which is conceived in her is of the Holy Spirit' (Matthew 1:20).

THE EVIDENCE OF DR. LUKE

Fittingly, it is Luke's Gospel which gives the fullest account of Christ's virginal conception — fittingly, because Luke himself was a medical doctor. He was known as 'Luke the beloved physician' (Colossians 4:14). When the angel Gabriel announced to Mary that she was to conceive and give birth to the very Son of God, Luke records that Mary, knowing the facts of life, asked 'How shall this be, since I have no husband?' (Luke 1:34). Gabriel then explained to Mary that the child she was to bear would be conceived without the instrumentality of a human father. He was to be conceived not naturally, but supernaturally, even miraculously, as 'The Holy Spirit will come upon you, and the power of the Most High will overshadow you; therefore the child to be born will be called holy, the Son of God' (Luke 1:35).

Sceptics and unbelievers have always cast — and continue to cast — scorn on the virgin birth of Christ. Christians, however, believe that the Bible means what is says and says what it means. They also concur with Luke 1:37 'For with God nothing will be impossible.' In dealing with the virgin birth, we are dealing with Omnipotence. Belief in Almighty God of necessity entails a belief in the miraculous. Let God be God! To discredit the virgin birth is to cast aspersions on the almighty power of God. Jeremiah 32:17 comes to mind here: 'Ah Lord God! It is thou who hast made the heavens and the earth by thy great power and by thy outstretched arm! Nothing is too hard for thee.'

THE IMPORTANCE OF THE VIRGIN BIRTH OF CHRIST

The virgin birth of Christ is included in all the major creeds of the Christian Faith — the summary statements defining core Christian doctrine. Why is this so? It is so because the virgin birth of Christ was a vital link in the divine plan of salvation. 'Christ Jesus came into the world to save sinners' (1 Timothy 1:15). To qualify as the Saviour of sinners, Christ had to be sinless Himself, not just in thought, word and deed, but in His very nature. Scripture affirms that He was. It was His conception by the Holy Spirit which ensures the sinlessness — the impeccability — of His nature. Had He been conceived through a human father, He would have inherited our human sin, for everyone born of a human father inherits the sinful nature of Adam and is in need of a Saviour from sin. When Christ died on the cross, He was treated as a sinner by God. Our sins were — as we shall see in another chapter — 'imputed' to Him. But Christ Himself was 'holy, blameless, unstained, separated from sinners' (Hebrews 7:26). His death was an atoning sacrifice for the sins of others. He died 'like that of a lamb without blemish or spot' (1 Peter 1:19). Christ's unique sinlessness uniquely qualified Him to be the Saviour of sinners — and His virgin birth — His conception by the Holy Spirit — ensured that the human nature of Christ was totally untainted by our human sin.

So, Christians believe that the Son of God truly became man, being begotten of the Holy Ghost and born of the Virgin Mary. They do so because the Bible tells us so. Those who do not hold to Christ's virgin birth can never be said to hold a Christian view of Christ. The alternatives to the virgin birth of Christ are unthinkable. If Christ was not virgin born, the Bible is untrue — yet the Bible is the Word of a 'God, who never lies' (Titus 1:2). If Christ was not virgin born, Mary was a fornicator. If Christ was not virgin born, He was a sinner. If Christ was not virgin born, we have no Saviour from our sin and will have to pay the price for it ourselves, in an eternal hell ... But Christ was virgin born, for the Bible tells us so. Christ alone — the God-man and the sinless one — is uniquely qualified to be the Saviour of all who put their trust in Him. He was, as the *Apostles' Creed* succinctly states, 'conceived by the Holy Spirit, born of the Virgin Mary, was crucified, died and buried ... '

Christ by highest heaven adored
Christ the everlasting Lord
Late in time behold Him come
Offspring of a virgin's womb
Veiled in flesh the Godhead see
Hail the incarnate Deity
Pleased as Man with men to dwell
Jesus our Immanuel.

(Charles Wesley 1707-1788)

QUESTIONS AND POINTS TO PONDER

1. There were those in the early church who were known as 'Docetists.' They denied the real humanity of Christ. Why did God have to become man? List some of the Scripture evidence which prove that Christ was truly human.

2. What comfort is there from knowing that Christ was and is truly human as well as divine?

3. The 'virgin birth' of Christ is in all the major Christian creeds. Is this 'majoring on minors'? Why does the virgin birth of Christ matter?

4. Theologians distinguish between the person of Christ and the work of Christ. But are the person and work of Christ inextricable?

5. 'Christ is the gospel and the gospel is Christ.'

CHAPTER FOUR

THAT HIS DEATH WAS A SACRIFICE TO GOD AND PROPITIATION FOR THE REMISSION OF SINS

BORN TO DIE

The emphasis of the Bible is not so much on the life of Christ, but the death of Christ — on 'Christ crucified' (1 Corinthians 1:23). The pages of the Bible are taken up, as regards space, not so much with Christ's incarnation but rather with His crucifixion. Why is this so? It is so because the sinner's salvation was achieved, not by Christ's living or teaching, but by His dying. Most unusually, Christ was born not to live but to die.

The Lord Jesus saw fit to bequeath a memorial of Himself for His followers in posterity. This memorial is known as the Lord's Supper. The memorial commemorates not His life but His death. In obedience to Christ's command, bread and wine are taken and consumed. The bread is broken — to remind us that Christ's body was broken on the cross of Calvary. The wine is poured — to recall that Christ's blood was shed at Calvary for the sinner's forgiveness. The bread is eaten, and a sip of wine is drunk, symbolising a personal partaking of the saving benefits of Christ's redeeming work.

The Lord's Supper and its symbolism thus enforces to us that Christ Himself would have His followers focus primarily not on His birth, miracles or teaching — wonderful and marvellous though all those were — but on His cross and its saving benefits. It is this which constitutes the heart of the gospel. Hence, one of the earliest ever Christian creeds had the mind of Christ when it summarised the heart of the Christian Faith and stated in summary 'that Christ died for our sins' (1 Corinthians 15:3). Likewise, with the Apostolic preaching of the gospel. The apostles focused on the Lord Jesus for sure but note the emphasis. They 'decided to know nothing among you except Jesus Christ and him *crucified*' (1 Corinthians 2:2, author's emphasis).

Although it was barbaric beyond words, death by crucifixion was not unusual in the first century Greco-Roman world. But Christ's death by crucifixion was totally unique and unparalleled, as Christ Himself is totally unique and unparalleled. His death was no ordinary death but a saving act of God. The Bible teaches that His death was a sacrifice to God and propitiation for the remission of sins.

THE CENTRALITY OF SACRIFICE

The Bible teaches that 'the wages of sin is death' (Romans 6:23). Sin against God could not be more serious. Sin against God cannot go unpunished by Him but has to be atoned for. How is it atoned for? Either by the punishment of the sinner himself, or by the punishment of a substitute — one who takes the place of the sinner. In His mercy, God Himself instituted the sacrificial system with the latter in mind. He ordained that a substitute could take the place of the sinner to spare and deliver the sinner from the punishment he deserved. The essence of this is encapsulated in Leviticus 17:11 where God explained to Moses 'For the life of the flesh is in the blood; and I have given it to you upon the altar to make atonement for your souls; for it is the blood that makes atonement, by reason of the life.'

The meaning behind the sacrificial system given by God is this. The sinner deserves death. But God ordained that an innocent animal could die in the place of the sinner on the sacrificial altar, in effect taking the punishment due to the sinner, thus releasing the sinner from sin's dreadful penalty.

Sacrifice was central to the Old Testament economy. The Old Testament sacrifices though all foreshadowed better things to come. The on-going sacrifices of the Old Testament era all pointed forward to Christ and His atoning death — the sacrifice of His sinless life which would fully atone for all His peoples' sins and render all sacrifice as obsolete, unnecessary and redundant.

THE SACRIFICE OF CHRIST

The Bible teaches that Christ's death was an atoning sacrifice — a sacrifice which, in contrast to the Old Testament sacrifices, atones for the believer's sins fully, finally, and for ever. 'He has appeared once for all at the end of the age to put away sin by the sacrifice of himself' (Hebrews 9:26). 'When Christ had offered for all time a single sacrifice for sins he sat down at the right hand of God' (Hebrews 10:12).

Furthermore, the Bible teaches that Christ's death was a *substitutionary* sacrifice — He took the place of the believing sinner; He died in their room and stead. He, the sinless One, bore the liability for the sins of others to exonerate and liberate them from that liability. 'He himself bore our sins in his body on the tree' (1 Peter 2:24). 'Christ having been offered once to bear the sins of many' (Hebrews 9:28).

PROPITIATION

If there is one word which encapsulates the meaning of the death of Christ, it is the word 'propitiation.' The Bible teaches that Christ's substitutionary sacrifice was a propitiation. To propitiate means to avert the wrath, to appease, to satisfy. A holy God has to punish sin. God is actually righteously angry with sinners for breaking His law and rebelling against Him. Every single infraction of God's law renders the law-breaker guilty and liable to pay the penalty for breaking God's law. Breaking God's law renders us liable to God's wrath — His holy indignation. The gospel however proclaims that Christ paid the penalty for the broken law on the sinner's behalf. 'He was wounded for *our* transgressions . . .' (Isaiah 53:5, author's emphasis). He 'was put to death for *our* trespasses' (Romans 4:25, author's emphasis). He turned aside the wrath of God which was due to the sinner, and He did so by taking it on Himself in full, at Calvary. 'He is the propitiation for our sins' (1 John 2:2 KJV). 'Herein is love, not that we loved God, but that He loved us and sent his Son to be the propitiation for our sins' (1 John 4:10). Through Christ alone the wrath of God which we deserve is turned aside; it is satisfied; it is averted; it is propitiated.

How do we explain the fact that when Christ suffered and died on Calvary's cross 'From the sixth hour there was darkness over all the land until the ninth hour. And about the ninth hour Jesus cried with a loud voice, "Eli, Eli, lama sabachthani?" that is, "My God, My God, why hast thou forsaken me?"' (Matthew 27:45,46 RSV)? We do so only by the fact that He was taking the place of the sinner and enduring the wrath of God that is the sinner's due. He was judged for our justification. He was punished to procure our pardon. He endured the darkness so that we might enjoy the light of God. He was separated from God so that we might be reconciled to God. He died so that we 'should not perish but have eternal life' (John 3:16). It is truly awful. Yet it is also awesomely wonderful. It is the very gospel of God Himself.

O Christ what burdens bowed Thy head
Our load was laid on Thee
Thou stoodest in the sinner's stead
Didst bear all ill for me
A victim led, Thy blood was shed
Now there's no load for me

The Holy One did hide His face
O Christ t'was hid from Thee

Dumb darkness wrapped Thy soul a space
The darkness due to me
But now that face of radiant grace
Shines forth in light on me.

(Ann Ross Cousin, 1824-1906)

THE REMISSION OF SINS

In 1 John 2:12 John writes the following simple, but very reassuring verse to his Christian readers: 'I am writing to you, little children, because your sins are forgiven for his sake.'

Christians are not necessarily 'good' people or even 'nice' people. But they are a forgiven people. They are sinners, but sinners who have been saved by the grace of God, in Christ, at Calvary. The forgiveness of sins is a uniquely Christian blessing. But can a Christian really make the claim that those sins of theirs which damn them, and impede their fellowship with a thrice holy God, are really all wiped off their account? Yes, they can. Why? Because Christ died for them. At Calvary He paid the penalty for their sins in full, so that they now have nothing at all to pay. 'In him we have redemption through his blood, the forgiveness of our trespasses, according to the riches of his grace' (Ephesians 1:7).

A Christian therefore has nothing to boast of intrinsically in him or herself. All we contribute to our salvation is our sins! No. A Christian owes everything to the grace of God. A Christian owes everything to the cross of Christ and the Christ of the cross.

So, Christians believe, know, and rejoice that Christ's death on the cross was a sacrifice to God and propitiation for the remission of sins. Christians vary in age, nationality, size, intellect etc. Yet the testimony of every Christian is the same: 'But far be it from me to glory except in the cross of our Lord Jesus Christ, by which the world has been crucified to me, and I to the world' (Galatians 6:14).

We sing the praise of Him who died
Of Him who died upon the cross
The sinner's hope let men deride
For this we count the world but loss.

Inscribed upon the cross we see
In shining letters 'God is love'
He bears our sins upon the tree
He brings us mercy from above.

(Thomas Kelly 1769-1855)

QUESTIONS AND POINTS TO PONDER

1. Sacrifice is central to both the Old and New Testament econo-
    mies. What is the biblical significance of sacrifice?

2. 'Those who fail to understand the cross of Christ in terms of a
    'propitiation' fail to understand both the nature of God Himself
    and the saving work of Christ.' Discuss.

3. Why, according to the Bible, are those who seek salvation in a way
    which by-passes the cross, in eternal peril?

4. 'I do not nullify the grace of God; for if justification were through
    the law, then Christ died to no purpose' (Galatians 2:21).

5. There is a disproportionate amount of space in the Gospels to the
    last week of the Saviour's life on earth. The Gospels have been
    described as 'passion narratives with extended introductions.'
    What does this emphasis of the Gospel writers imply?

6. 'Christians are not necessarily good people, but they are forgiven
    people.' Is it arrogant to profess that we are sure that our sins are
    forgiven and that we have peace with God?

CHAPTER FIVE

CHRISTIANS BELIEVE THAT CHRIST WAS RAISED FROM THE DEAD

THE RESURRECTION OF CHRIST

The earliest ever Christian creed, that is, the earliest ever basic summary of non-negotiable Christian fundamentals, goes as follows: 'that Christ died for our sins in accordance with the Scriptures, that He was buried, that *He was raised on the third day* in accordance with the Scriptures (1 Corinthians 15:3,4). We thus come to the resurrection of the Lord Jesus Christ.

This first Christian creed encapsulates plain facts of history as well as theology. The Son of God was indeed crucified, and after this His body was lovingly buried. But three days later, the Scripture records reveal that Christ conquered the grave. He rose from the dead and was subsequently seen, heard, touched and worshipped by many. 'This Jesus God raised up, and of that we are all witnesses' (Acts 2:32). The Christian Faith is thus a resurrection faith. It is founded on a risen Saviour — one who overcame the tomb and is living and life-giving today.

STUBBORN SCRIPTURE FACTS

The stubborn facts of Christ's empty tomb and His various post resurrection appearances have never been explained away by even the harshest of critics and sceptics. This is because they cannot be explained away. Take as a case study the Apostle Peter. In a moment of cowardice, he once denied His Master Jesus, swearing that he never knew Him. In the first ever Christian sermon however, the same Peter proclaimed fearlessly to a vast crowd in Jerusalem 'this Jesus, delivered up according to the definite plan and foreknowledge of God, you crucified and killed by the hands of lawless men. *But God raised him up,* having loosed the pangs of death, because it was not possible for him to be held by it' (Acts 2:23,24, author's emphasis). And Peter went on to confirm '*This Jesus God raised up,* and of that we are all witnesses' (v. 32, author's emphasis). How do we account for and explain Peter's transformation apart from the historical fact of the resurrection of Christ? Peter himself was eventually martyred for his belief in the risen Saviour. He surely would not have been as brave as he was and undergone such endeavours for Christ if, in his heart of hearts, he knew that Christ was still dead. Also, an awkward question for sceptics is 'Where is Christ's body?' If Peter was preaching a lie, the simplest thing would have been to produce Christ's corpse, shut Peter up for good and quash the growth of the Christian church in its early days. No such thing ever happened. It did not happen as it could not happen, for Christ had risen from the dead. 'The Lord has risen indeed, and has appeared to Simon! [Peter]' (Luke 24:34). ' . . . He appeared to Cephas, [Peter] then to the twelve' (1 Corinthians 15:5).

'Christ did truly rise again from the dead and took again His body, with flesh, bones, and all things appertaining to the perfection of man's nature; wherewith He ascended into heaven and there sitteth, until He return to judge all men at the last day' (*39 Articles,* chapter IV).

THE RING OF TRUTH

Just as Peter's transformation contradicts and confounds those who are sceptical about Christ's resurrection, so also does His first resurrection appearance. John records that 'on the first day of the week Mary Mag'dalene came to the tomb early . . . ' (John 20:1). She was to visit the tomb of the One she supposed had been cruelly killed and was now dead. But Mary Magdalene was to meet the risen Saviour! He was alive! She saw, heard, and touched Him. 'Jesus said to her "Mary." She turned and said to him in Hebrew, "Rab-bo'ni!" (which means Teacher)' (John 20:18). Why does this confound the sceptics? Because of the low status of women in the first century. They were considered to be unreliable. They could not give evidence in court. Mary's witness would be considered as doubly unreliable, as not only was she a woman, but she had something of a disreputable past. But this confirms the truth of Christ's resurrection! If a creative writer had invented it, he would not have said that Christ appeared first to Mary Magdalene. He would have said to the high priest, the Emperor or perhaps a Roman centurion . . . But Mary Magdalene? It shows that we are dealing with historical truth and not invented myth.

So, the risen Saviour appeared to individuals — to Peter, Mary, and others. Were they all deluded? Were they all hallucinating? Hardened unbelievers would like to think so. First Corinthians 15:6 though testifies that the risen Christ once 'appeared to more than five hundred brethren at one time, most of whom are still alive.' Five hundred people who hallucinated at the exact same time? Hardly. There is no excuse for unbelief when the hard, biblical evidence for Christ's resurrection is considered honestly. Christians, who meet together on the first day of the week — the day of Christ's resurrection — to worship the risen Christ, have every reason to believe that Christ was raised from the dead.

Jesus Christ is risen today, Hallelujah!
Our triumphant holy day, Hallelujah!
Who did once upon the cross, Hallelujah!
Suffer to redeem our loss, Hallelujah!

Hymns of praise then let us sin
Unto Christ our heavenly King

Who endured the cross and grave
Sinners to redeem and save

But the anguish He endured
Our salvation hath procured
Now above the sky He's King
Where the angels ever sing, Hallelujah!

(Lyra Davidica b. 1708)

THE CONSEQUENCES OF THE RESURRECTION

The resurrection of Christ is an historical fact. The resurrection of Christ is also an historic fact. Along with His incarnation, it is *the* most significant fact of all history. So, what does Christ's bodily resurrection signify? Why is it so important?

Firstly, the resurrection of Christ validates all the stupendous claims that He made. Christ predicted His own resurrection and His prediction came true. Jesus foretold His disciples on more than one occasion 'Behold, we are going up to Jerusalem, and the Son of man will be delivered to the chief priests and the scribes, and they will condemn him to death, and deliver him to the Gentiles; and they will mock him, and spit upon him and scourge him, and kill him; *and after three days he will rise*' (Mark 10:33,34, author's emphasis).

Secondly, the resurrection of Christ is the final proof of His absolute deity. He is the Son of God and God the Son — 'designated Son of God in power according to the Spirit of holiness by his resurrection from the dead' (Romans 1:4). Christ conquered the grave. If we are united to Christ by faith, we too will conquer the grave. Jesus said, 'I am the resurrection and the life; he who believes in me, though he die, yet shall he live, and whoever lives and believes in me shall never die' (John 11:25,26).

Thirdly, the resurrection of Christ is God the Father's endorsement of His Son's atoning death on the cross. Jesus 'became obedient unto death, even death on a cross. Therefore, God has highly exalted him' (Philippians 2:8,9). He was 'put to death for our trespasses and raised for our justification' (Romans 4:25). He paid the debt of our sins in full on Good Friday. God the Father accepted the payment, and on Easter Sunday expressed His 'Received with thanks' by raising His Son from the dead.

Fourthly, the resurrection of Christ is a foretaste of the Christian's own resurrection at the last day. Death is not the end for the believer. The grave is not the end for the believer. 'Christ has been raised from the dead, the first fruits of those who have fallen asleep' (1 Corinthians 15:20). This points us forward to the resurrection at the last day, when Christ comes again in power and great glory:

'At the resurrection, believers, being raised up in glory, shall be openly acknowledged and acquitted in the day of judgment, and made perfectly blessed in the full enjoying of God to all eternity' (*Shorter Catechism*, Q. 38).

The resurrection of Christ. It is the Fact of all facts, historical and historic. Christians believe the testimony of the Bible that Christ was raised from the dead. And Christians know, enjoy, and rejoice in the presence of this living Saviour day by day.

> *I serve a risen Saviour, He's in the world today*
> *I know that He is living, whatever men may say*
> *I see His hand of mercy, I hear His voice of cheer*
> *And just the time I need Him, He's always near.*

> *Rejoice, rejoice, O Christian, lift up your voice and sing*
> *Eternal hallelujahs to Jesus Christ the King!*
> *The hope of all who seek Him, the help of all who find*
> *None other is so loving, so good and kind.*

He lives! He lives! Christ Jesus lives today!

He walks with me and talks with me along life's narrow way

He lives! He lives! Salvation to impart!

You ask me how I know He lives? He lives within my heart!

(A.H. Ackley 1887-1960)

QUESTIONS AND POINTS TO PONDER

1. 'The resurrection of Christ is the most attested fact in history' (Thomas Arnold). List as many Scriptural and non-Scriptural evidences as you can for the resurrection of Christ.

2. Why do the Gospel accounts of Christ's resurrection have the 'ring of truth' to them, which shows that they are fact and not fiction?

3. What, according to the Bible, are the consequences of Christ's resurrection?

4. 'If Christ has not been raised, your faith is futile and you are still in your sins' (1 Corinthians 15:17).

CHAPTER SIX

CHRISTIANS BELIEVE THAT CHRIST ASCENDED TO THE RIGHT HAND OF GOD AND IS NOW THE ALL-SUFFICIENT HIGH PRIEST OF HIS PEOPLE

THE INCOMPARABLE CHRIST

The uniqueness of the Christian Faith stems from the uniqueness of the Lord Jesus Christ who lies at the heart of the Christian Faith. Scripture reveals Him as the God-man and only Saviour of sinners, as He only is qualified to be the Saviour of sinners.

In-line with His unique Person, Scripture reveals that Christ both entered into our world in a unique way and exited from our world in a unique way. As we have seen, Christ entered our world through being 'conceived by the Holy Spirit and born of the virgin Mary.' Then, having accomplished the eternal redemption of His people, Christ exited from the world by ascending miraculously back to heaven. Peter explains and exclaims that Jesus Christ 'has gone into heaven and is at the right hand of God, with angels, authorities, and powers subject to him' (1 Peter 3:22). Peter himself was actually present — along with the remaining disciples — to witness Christ's ascension back to heaven. The Bible relates that 'as they were looking on . . . a cloud took Him out of their sight' (Acts 1:9).

ASCENSION AND GLORIFICATION

Mark concludes his account of Jesus' earthly ministry very succinctly when he says how 'the Lord Jesus . . . was taken up into heaven, and sat down at the right hand of God' (Mark 16:19). The expression 'the right hand of God' refers to the place of highest honour, eminence and pre-eminence. It also refers to the place of supreme authority, from which the Lord Jesus directs and controls all things for the blessing of His people and the building of His church. Having fulfilled His mission on earth 'God has highly exalted him and bestowed on him the name [rank] which is above every name' (Philippians 2:9). Jesus was 'crowned with glory and honor because of the suffering of death' (Hebrews 2:9).

The head that once was crowned with thorns
Is crowned with glory now
A royal diadem adorns
The mighty Victor's brow

The highest place that heaven affords
Is His by sovereign right
The King of kings and Lord of lords
And heaven's eternal light.

(Thomas Kelly 1769-1855)

When we consider Christ's ascension, we are concerned with His state of exaltation. Christ underwent a transition from a state of humiliation — His birth in a stable, His rejection and crucifixion — to a state of greatness. The *Shorter Catechism* states: 'Christ's exaltation consisteth in His rising again from the dead on the third day, in ascending up into heaven, in sitting at the right hand of God the Father, and in coming to judge the world at the last day' (Q. 28).

Christ occupies this exalted state at this very moment.

THE ON-GOING WORK OF CHRIST

Although Christ is currently enthroned in heaven, Scripture teaches that He is presently far from inactive on behalf of His people, for He is now their all-sufficient great high priest. Paradoxically, the Bible teaches that Christ's ministry is both finished and on-going.

Christians rejoice in an accomplished redemption — the 'finished work of Christ.' Moments before Christ finally died on the cross, 'he said, "It is finished"; and he bowed his head and gave up his spirit' (John 19:30). If we belong to Jesus, our redemption has been secured. 'When he had made purification for sins, he sat down at the right hand of the Majesty on high' (Hebrews 1:3). Christ's work is finished! Yet we have also to consider the unfinished work of Christ — His ongoing intercession for His people:

> 'Tis finished!' On the Cross He said
>
> In agonies and blood
>
> 'Tis finished!' now He lives to plead
>
> Before the face of God.

(James Deck 1803-84)

Wonderfully, Scripture reveals that Christ's presence at God's right hand is for the benefit of His people. 'Christ has entered . . . into heaven itself, now to appear in the presence of God on our behalf' (Hebrews 9:24). At God's right hand, Jesus acts as our great high priest. Jesus intercedes for His own — and His prayers always prevail. His presence and prayers keep us eternally in the good of His finished work of redemption. It is 'Christ Jesus, who died, yes, who was raised from the dead, who is at the right hand of God, *who indeed intercedes for us*' (Romans 8:34, author emphasis). Here is solace for His people. We have a Friend and Advocate in the highest place. 'Consequently he is able for all time to save those who draw near to God through him, since he always lives to make intercession for them' (Hebrews 7:25).

OUR GREAT HIGH PRIEST

The Lord Jesus Christ is now the all-sufficient great High Priest of His people. '. . . We have a great high priest who has passed through the heavens, Jesus, the Son of God' (Hebrews 4:14). His sacrifice is complete. His intercession is on-going.

'How doth Christ execute the office of a priest?'

'Christ executeth the office of a priest in His once offering up of Himself a sacrifice to satisfy divine justice and reconcile us to God; and in making continual intercession for us' (*Shorter Catechism*, Q. 25).

J. Packer says the following about Christ's intercession — possibly a neglected facet of His ministry to His people: 'Christ's priestly intercession is a royal intervention from the throne, an intervention rooted in the fact that He, the king, is present with God as the advocate of His people, the eternally effective propitiation for their sins in virtue of His once-for-all sacrifice. We should therefore define Christ's intercession as that heavenly activity, of whatever kind, whereby He makes sure that all who come to God through Him, pleading His name, trusting Him for forgiveness, access, grace to help in time of need, and ultimate glory, will not be disappointed. The New Testament does not encourage us to speculate as to the exact nature of this activity, but rather to rejoice in the knowledge that, whatever precise form it takes, it is certainly and infallibly efficacious' (*God's Words*, p. 118).

So, Christians believe that their Saviour, the Lord Jesus Christ ascended to the right hand of God and is now the all-sufficient high priest of His people. Thank God that this is so!

Before the throne of God above
I have a strong a perfect plea
A great High Priest, whose Name is love
Who ever lives and pleads for me.

My name is graven on His hands
My name is written on His heart
I know that while in heaven He stands
No tongue can bid me thence depart.

(Charitie Lees De Chenez 1841-1923)

QUESTIONS AND POINTS TO PONDER

1. In what way may Christ's work be said to be finished? On-going?

2. Scripture states that Christ is currently seated 'at the right hand of God.' What does this expression mean? 'God is spirit' (John 4:24) and has no 'hands'?

3. Do you think that Christ's current high priestly ministry is a somewhat neglected facet of His saving work for His people?

4. Christ both came into the world miraculously and exited from the world miraculously. In what other ways is Christ absolutely unique?

5. 'The uniqueness of the Christian Faith stems from the uniqueness of the Christ Who is at the heart of the Christian Faith.'

CHRISTIANS BELIEVE THAT CHRIST WILL COME AGAIN TO RECEIVE THEM TO HIMSELF AND TO SET UP HIS KINGDOM ON EARTH

THE PROMISE OF HIS COMING

The very last recorded words of Christ in the Bible are these: 'Surely I am coming soon' (Revelation 22:20). World history will yet prove to be 'His story.' Contrary to external appearances, history is not random, haphazard, or uncertain, because, according to the Bible, the goal of all history is the Second Coming of the Lord Jesus Christ. Jesus is coming again! We are told that there are some 318 references to the Second Coming of Christ in holy Scripture.

When the Saviour faced His impending arrest and crucifixion, the atmosphere amongst His disciples was understandably foreboding. But the light of Jesus pierced the gloom. He promised them a glorious home in His Father's house, and He also promised that 'I will come again and will take you to myself, that where I am you may be also' (John 14:3).

THE PROSPECT OF HIS COMING

The Second Coming of Christ is the most thrilling prospect conceivable for all those who know Him as their Saviour. Small wonder that throughout the ages Christians have always prayed 'Maranatha' — 'Come, Lord Jesus!'

(Revelation 22:20). For when Jesus comes to reign, we shall be raised up to glory and immortality 'and so we shall always be with the Lord' (1 Thessalonians 4:17). In the nearer presence of our Saviour, we shall be eternally saved, eternally safe and eternally satisfied:

'For ever with the Lord!'

Amen, so let it be!

Life from the dead is in that word

Tis immortality

Here in the body pent

Absent from Him I roam

Yet nightly pitch my moving tent

A day's march nearer home.

My Father's home on high

Home of my soul, how near

At times to faith's foreseeing eye

Thy golden gates appear!

Ah then my spirit faints

To reach the land I love

The bright inheritance of saints

Jerusalem above.

(James Montgomery 1171-1854)

Jesus will most certainly come again. The Bible tells us so. Whilst Scripture forbids us from setting dates for this momentous event on the divine calendar — 'But of that day or that hour no one knows . . . ' (Matthew 24:36) — it does enjoin us to be ready for that Day. And the way to be ready is to be the friend of Christ — to know Him as our Friend and Saviour. 'Therefore you also must be ready; for the Son of man is coming at an hour you do not expect' (Matthew 24:44).

The Lord is coming by and by
Be ready when He comes!
He comes from His fair home on high
Be ready when He comes!
He is the Lord our Righteousness
And comes His chosen ones to bless
And at His Father's throne confess
Be ready when He comes.

(Elisha Hoffman 1838-1929)

Jesus will come again and gloriously receive His people — His redeemed — to Himself. His word is sure. 'I will come again and will take you to myself, that where I am you may be also' (John 14:3). But there is a further facet to Christ's coming again in glory, which we shall consider under the heading of:

THE PURPOSE OF HIS COMING

Paradoxically, according to Scripture, Jesus both reigns — He is currently enthroned at God's right hand — and Jesus shall yet reign. He is coming again to set up His eternal kingdom here on earth. Christians are taught by the Saviour to pray 'Thy kingdom come.' And one day this prayer will be answered fully. Revelation 11:15 gives us a prophetic foresight and insight into the time on God's calendar still future when 'The kingdom of the world has become the kingdom of our Lord and of his Christ, and he shall reign for ever and ever.'

The Second Coming of Christ will contrast greatly with His first coming. Christ's first coming was, humanly speaking, an obscure event, witnessed only by His earthly parents and some anonymous shepherds in Bethlehem. Christ's Second Coming however will be in power and great glory. Jesus said, 'For as the lightning flashes and lights up the sky from one side to the other, so will be the Son of man in his day' (Luke 17:24). 'Behold, he is coming with the clouds, and every eye will see him' (Revelation 1:7).

Jesus is coming to put right everything that is wrong in this fallen world. When He comes again, He will destroy all the enemies of God and eradicate all that is incompatible with God's righteousness and love. 'For he must reign until he has put all his enemies under his feet' (1 Corinthians 15:25). When Christ comes again, His people will undergo a transformation — given new, glorious bodies free from our current handicaps and limitations. And even the universe itself will be transformed, for He will eradicate all vestiges of the Fall. This is the Christian's 'blessed hope' (Titus 2:13), that is, confident expectation: living in redeemed bodies on a redeemed earth in the glorious kingdom of the King of kings. 'According to his promise we wait new heavens and a new earth in which righteousness dwells' (2 Peter 3:13). 'And the effect of righteousness will be peace, and the result of righteousness, quietness and trust for ever' (Isaiah 32:17). Through the love of God our Saviour, all will be well!

MARANATHA!

To date, some two thousand years plus have separated the first and second comings of Christ. The question is begged 'Why does He appear to delay His coming?' The answer of the Bible is 'So that sinners might hear the gospel and be saved.' Some of Peter's last written words were words of explanation that 'The Lord is not slow about his promise as some count slowness, but is forbearing toward you, not wishing that any should perish, but that all should reach repentance' (2 Peter 3:9).

Jesus explained, 'This gospel of the kingdom will be preached throughout the whole world, as a testimony to all nations; and then the end will come' (Matthew 24:14). The Bible divides time into two: this fallen age and the glorious age to come. Whilst this age is a fallen age, it is yet also a day of grace. The gospel of salvation is being preached. Sinners are being saved. Modern technology is such that the gospel is being heard in ever expanding avenues and horizons. One day however, the very last one of God's elect will hear, believe, and be saved. 'And then the end will come.' Jesus will come again! He will come again to receive His people to Himself and set up His kingdom on earth. Hasten the day! The Christian's prospect is brighter than bright. Our future is as bright as the promises of God!

Jesus is coming! Sing the glad word
Coming for those He redeemed by His blood
Coming to reign as the glorified Lord!
Jesus is coming again!

Jesus is coming! His saints to release
Coming to give to the weary world peace
Sinning and sighing and sorrow shall cease
Jesus is coming again!

Jesus is coming, is coming again
Jesus is coming again
Shout the glad tidings o'er mountain and plain
Jesus is coming again.
(Daniel Webster Whittle 1840-1901)

QUESTIONS AND POINTS TO PONDER

1. What practical affects does, or should, the prospect of Christ's second coming have on our lives? (see 2 Peter 3:11).

2. Is there a happy medium between those churches which over stress Christ's second coming and those which rarely, if ever, mention the subject at all?

3. What is the main thing we have to do to be prepared for Christ's coming in glory?

CHAPTER EIGHT

CHRISTIANS BELIEVE THAT IN CONSEQUENCE OF THE FALL OF ADAM, MAN BECAME 'LOST WITHOUT STRENGTH' AND AT ENMITY WITH GOD

In any sphere of life, a right diagnosis of a problem always precedes the correct solution and cure of that problem. If the problem is ignored, the situation remains unfixed and even exacerbates. So, if we ignore a strange noise in the engine of our car, we may find ourselves stranded away from home. If we refrain from seeking medical advice when we feel unwell, our condition may deteriorate into something more serious. If we ignore a virus on our computer, we might end up losing all the data on it and suffer the consequent stress and inconvenience. Examples could be multiplied.

MALADY AND REMEDY

When it comes to our eternal welfare — our relationship and standing with God Himself — a right diagnosis of our condition is absolutely vital. If we ignore our condition, or if we leave it undiagnosed, detrimental eternal consequences ensue. Unless we see ourselves as sinners who are not right with God, and unless we realise — or are enabled to realise — our need of a Saviour, we will never seek salvation — we will not see the need for God's gracious solution to our plight in the Lord Jesus Christ and His death on the cross. Jesus said, 'Those who are well have no need of a physician, but those who are sick; I came not to call the righteous, but sinners' (Mark 2:17).

IN THE DIVINE CONSULTING ROOM

The Bible gives a very different diagnosis of our human condition from the flattering 'self-esteem' and 'feel-good gurus' which are around today. The Bible says that we are sinners by nature and practice, and as such we are out of fellowship with God our Maker. And we are sinners because we are descendants of Adam, our first ancestor. He sinned against God, and we have inherited his fallen human nature with its dreadful and damnable consequences. 'Sin came into the world through one man [Adam] . . . and so death [physical and spiritual] spread to all men because all men sinned' (Romans 5:12).

'They (our first parents) being the root of all mankind, the guilt of this sin was imputed; and the same death in sin, and corrupted nature, conveyed to all their posterity descending from them by ordinary generation' (*Westminster Confession of Faith*, Chapter 6, paragraph III).

The Bible's diagnosis of our condition by nature then is unflattering but crystal clear: 'all have sinned and fall short of the glory of God' (Romans 3:23). The consequence of Adam's fall — and our fall by and in him — are many and various, as they are dire, deadly, and damnable. But here we major on two prominent ones.

TOTAL INABILITY

Firstly, in consequence of the fall of Adam, we are 'lost without strength.' The expression comes from Romans 5:6 in the King James version of the Bible: 'For when we were yet without strength, in due time Christ died for the ungodly.' Alternative translations say 'While we were still weak, at the right time Christ died for the ungodly' (RSV) and 'When we were still powerless, Christ

died for the ungodly' (NIV). All the translations make the same point that sin
has put us into a hopeless and helpless state. We are lost and separated from
God, and in and of ourselves are unable to find our way home back to God.
We are unable in and of ourselves to change our condition and predicament.
We are unable to wipe out the guilty record of our sins. We are unable to live
a life which is perfectly pleasing to God. We cannot weave a robe of perfect
righteousness which fits us for His holy presence. Sin has thus disabled us
and deadened us. By nature, we are spiritually sick, disabled, and powerless.
The diagnosis precedes the cure. 'The whole head is sick, and the whole heart
faint. From the sole of the foot even to the head, there is no soundness in
it, but bruises and sores and bleeding wounds; they are not pressed out, or
bound up, or softened with oil' (Isaiah 1:5,6 RSV).

The theological term for our condition by nature of being powerless to
save ourselves is 'total inability.' By nature, we cannot save ourselves, and
apart from divine grace and the working of God's Spirit, we do not even want
to be saved.

'Man, by his fall into a state of sin, hath wholly lost all ability of will to
any spiritual good accompanying salvation: so as a natural man, being altogether averse from that good, and dead in sin, is not able, by his own strength,
to convert himself or prepare himself thereunto' (*Westminster Confession of
Faith*, Chapter 9, III).

Secondly, as a result of Adam's fall, very sadly, by nature, we are in a state of:

TOTAL ENMITY

Our sin separates us from God. It is our sin which impedes our enjoying
the fellowship with God which is our chief end. 'Your iniquities have made a
separation between you and your God, and your sins have hid his face from
you so that he does not hear' (Isaiah 59:2).

Most formidably and fearfully of all, our sin puts us under the wrath of
God — His righteous indignation. God is holy. He reacts to sin with revulsion.

He has to punish sin. Breaking His law brings down on us the curse of the law. Even in this life law breakers have to pay a penalty. Breaking God's law renders us liable to paying an eternal penalty — suffering His wrath for ever. We are thus 'by nature children of wrath, like the rest of mankind' (Ephesians 2:3). The bad news comes first. In summary, we are all by nature at enmity with God.

GOOD NEWS!

It is against the above dark background that the light of the gospel comes to us as the good news that it is. Yes, we are unable to save ourselves — but God in His mercy sent Jesus to be the Saviour of sinners. 'We have seen and testify that the Father has sent his Son as the Savior of the world' (1 John 4:14). In Christ alone, and by the shedding of His blood on Calvary, we find the forgiveness of all our sins and a perfect righteousness — His own righteousness — freely given to us, received by faith. We cannot save ourselves, but He can, and does!

Also, yes, we are indeed at enmity with God. But 'Jesus . . . delivers us from the wrath to come' (1 Thessalonians 1:10). He does so because He took God's wrath against our sins when He died in our place on the cross. Jesus is the great reconciling Saviour.

RECONCILIATION

'Reconciliation' is a key gospel word. To reconcile means to bring together two parties that previously were at odds — that were at enmity. The gospel proclaims that 'in Christ God was reconciling the world to himself, not counting their trespasses against them' (2 Corinthians 5:18). The exhortation of the gospel to sinners is therefore 'We beseech you on behalf of Christ, be reconciled to God' (2 Corinthians 5:20), that is, avail yourself of Christ's reconciliatory work on Calvary's cross, for 'Christ also died for sins once for all, the righteous for the unrighteous, that he might bring us to God' (1 Peter 3:18). It is through the crucified Saviour that sinners at enmity with God find peace with God. It is via the cross of Christ and the Christ of the cross that our fellowship with God is restored.

So, in conclusion, the bad news always precedes the good. The diagnosis always precedes the cure. Before we can build high, we must dig down, and lay a foundation. The Bible teaches that in consequence of the fall of Adam, man became 'lost without strength' and at enmity with God. This is the necessary backcloth which precedes coming to and cleaving to the One who 'came to seek and to save the lost' (Luke 19:10).

How sad our state by nature is!
Our sin how deep it stains!
And Satan binds our captive minds
Fast in his slavish chains.

But there's a voice of sovereign grace
Sounds from the sacred Word –
Ho! Ye despairing sinners come
And trust upon the Lord.

My soul obeys the almighty call
And runs to this relief
I would believe Thy promise Lord
O help my unbelief.

To the dear fountain of thy blood
Incarnate God I fly
Here let me wash my guilty soul
From crimes of deepest dye.

A guilty, weak and helpless wretch
On thy kind arms I fall
Be Thou my strength and righteousness
My Jesus and my all.

(Isaac Watts 1674-1748)

QUESTIONS AND POINTS TO PONDER

1. Why is it necessary to have a biblical view of our human nature?

2. 'Unless we really are sinners, the cross of Christ makes no sense.' Discuss.

3. How does the Bible's diagnosis of our human condition differ from modern views of the human condition?

4. If we are unable to believe in Jesus in and of ourselves, is our condition hopeless? And why is the gospel to be preached if we are, in and of ourselves, unable to believe in Jesus?

5. 'He who would build high must first dig deep.' What is the connection between that statement and the Bible's diagnosis of and remedy for our human condition?

CHAPTER NINE

CHRISTIANS BELIEVE IN THE NEED OF THE HOLY SPIRIT'S WORK IN BOTH REGENERATION AND SANCTIFICATION

BIRTH AND REBIRTH

Our physical lives begin when we are conceived and subsequently born. Likewise, our spiritual lives as Christians begin when we are born again. The term 'born again Christian' is actually a tautology, akin to 'a round circle,' for to be a Christian is to have undergone a spiritual rebirth — being made alive to God, our sin and God's promise of salvation in Christ. This new birth is absolutely indispensable, for Jesus Himself said 'Truly, truly I say to you, unless one is born anew [literally, 'from above'], he cannot see the kingdom of God' (John 3:3), and 'Truly, truly, I say to you, unless one is born of water and the Spirit, he cannot enter the kingdom of God' (John 3:5). The latter is referred to by Paul as 'the washing of regeneration and renewal in the Holy Spirit' (Titus 3:5).

Just as we had no say in our physical birth — we were totally passive in it all — likewise with our spiritual rebirth. We can no more give ourselves spiritual life than we gave ourselves physical life and decided to come into the world. No. New life in Christ is explained solely by the secret and mysterious work of the Holy Spirit in an individual's heart and soul, implanting new life in them, raising them from spiritual death, and turning them to God in Christ.

FROM DEATH TO LIFE

In our previous chapter we considered that we are powerless to save ourselves. We can go even further than this and say that the Bible states that by nature we are spiritually dead — dead to God, dead to our lost plight, and dead to our need of Christ. But all of this changes when the Holy Spirit works in our hearts and bestows on us new life. Ephesians 2:1 and 2 describes the experience of every Christian when it says 'And you he made alive, when you were dead through the trespasses and sins in which you once walked, following the course of this world, following the prince of the power of the air, the spirit that is now at work in the sons of disobedience.' Christian conversion entails being made alive spiritually.

REGENERATION

The technical term for this new life which we are considering is 'regeneration.' Regeneration refers to the implanting of new life, by God's Spirit, in the human soul.

'Regeneration . . . is that divine act by which the sinner is endowed with new spiritual life, and by which the principle of that new life is first called into action' (Berkhof, *Systematic Theology*, p. 467).

Considering that every person is born spiritually dead, and thus incapable of believing, new life in Christ can be explained solely by the work of the Holy Spirit. It can be explained, but it cannot be explained away, as there is a mystery about the way of God with His creatures. Jesus said 'The wind blows where it wills, and you hear the sound of it, but you do not know whence it comes or whither it goes; so it is with everyone who is born of the Spirit' (John 3:8). We cannot see the wind, but we can observe its effects — whistling in the trees, rustling the leaves etc. Similarly, we cannot see the Holy Spirit giving new life, but we can observe His effects. These are a conviction of our sin and lost plight, a turning to Christ and a cleaving to Him as our own personal

Saviour, and a subsequent change of life revealed in a love for God's Word and a desire to live for Christ, a desire for fellowship with other Christians and a desire to please and serve God as best as a saved sinner is able.

REDEMPTION ACCOMPLISHED AND APPLIED

The Holy Spirit then is indispensable in relation to Christian salvation. The redemption procured by Christ is put into an individual's actual possession when the Holy Spirit applies that work of redemption to their heart and soul. We cannot say or dictate how the Holy Spirit works, but invariably He works through the preaching of the gospel. Through the preaching of Christ crucified, the Holy Spirit enlightens our minds and draws us to Christ and nurtures in us saving faith in Him.

In summary, the Holy Spirit of God is absolutely essential if we are to be born again — if we are to benefit eternally from the redemption God has provided in Christ. Salvation is a matter of a redemption both divinely accomplished and divinely applied. We cannot give ourselves new life. Jesus said, 'It is the Spirit that gives life, the flesh is of no avail' (John 6:63).

'All those whom God hath predestined unto life, and those only, He is pleased, in His appointed and accepted time, effectually to call, by His Word and Spirit, out of that state of sin and death, in which they are by nature, to grace and salvation, by Jesus Christ; enlightening their minds spiritually and savingly to understand the things of God, taking away their heart of stone, and giving unto them a heart of flesh, renewing their wills, and, by His almighty power, determining them to that which is good, and effectually drawing them to Jesus Christ: yet so, as they come most freely, being made wiling by His grace.

This effectual call is of God's free and special grace alone, not from anything at all foreseen in man, who is altogether passive therein, until, being quickened and renewed by the Holy Spirit, he is thereby enabled to answer this call, and to embrace the grace offered and conveyed in it' (*Westminster Confession of Faith*, chapter 10, I and II).

> *Eternal Spirit! We confess*
> *And sing the wonders of Thy grace*
> *Thy power conveys our blessings down*
> *From God the Father and the Son.*
>
> *Enlightened by Thy heavenly ray*
> *Our shades and darkness turn to day*
> *Thine inward teachings make us know*
> *Our danger and our refuge too.*
>
> (Isaac Watts 1674-1748)

We have need of the Holy Spirit to commence the Christian life. And the Bible also teaches that we need the Holy Spirit to continue the Christian life. To this latter aspect we now turn.

CHAPTER TEN

CHRISTIANS BELIEVE IN THE NEED OF THE HOLY SPIRIT'S WORK IN SANCTIFICATION

We have considered how the Holy Spirit of God — the third Person of the Trinity — is indispensable if we are to commence the Christian life. Scripture however also reveals that the Holy Spirit is also indispensable if we are to continue the Christian life. The Christian's life on earth is a 'life in the Spirit.' It is He who empowers the Christian to live for God. It is He who enables the Christian to live a life pleasing to God, and not be dragged down by the wiles and ways of the world, the flesh and the devil, 'for he who is in you is greater than he who is in the world' (1 John 4:4).

The Holy Spirit enables the Christian to progress in the Christian life. Pilgrims should make progress! The Holy Spirit enables us to gradually become more holy, that is to become more and more conformed to the image of Christ. In a nutshell, the Holy Spirit is responsible for the Christian's progressive sanctification. Paradoxically, a Christian is both already sanctified — we have been set apart by God for God — and a Christian is being sanctified — God's Spirit is still at work in our hearts, gradually refining us and ripening in us the fruit of the Spirit — and a Christian will yet be perfectly sanctified, for in the age to come we will be completely free from the sin which mars us in the present age. We come therefore to the matter of the Christ's present sanctification.

SANCTIFICATION

'What is sanctification?'

'Sanctification is the work of God's free grace, whereby we are renewed in the whole man after the image of God and are enabled more and more to die unto sin and live unto righteousness' (*Shorter Catechism*, Q. 35).

Lawson's explanatory comment again here is very helpful: 'Sanctification means making a person holy. It is here said to be a *work*, because it is done, not at once, but gradually, and a work of grace because it proceeds from God's undeserved goodness and is wrought in us from first to last by His own Spirit. It consists in our being made like to God — that is, in gradually learning to hate and cease from sin, and to love and practise holiness; and this is called a renewing, because it is restoring us to the state in which we were at first.'

The Holy Spirit of God is a divine resource available to every Christian, not just to a spiritual elite. Every Christian is indwelt by God's Holy Spirit. Paul wrote reminding some believers in Corinth who were far from perfect 'Do you not know that your body is a temple of the Holy Spirit within you, which you have from God? You are not your own; you were bought with a price. So glorify God in your body' (1 Corinthians 6:19,20). And in Ephesians 5:18 he commands all Christians to 'be filled with the Spirit.' This suggests that there are degrees in the Spirit's filling. This fullness though is there for the asking, when we realise our emptiness and need, and seek the Lord, confessing our weakness and dependence on Him for our Christian life and service.

GOD HASN'T FINISHED WITH ME YET!

Every Christian then is something of a work in progress. As the apocryphal sign on a garage had it: WORKSHOP DOWNSTAIRS. SHOW ROOM UPSTAIRS. Earth is the workshop, but heaven is the showroom! We will always have to battle with our sinful nature in this life. The Bible does not teach sinless perfection. In this fallen world and in our fallen state, sanctification will never be complete, and we will never be able to say that we have 'arrived.' But we do not battle in our own strength. 'God . . . gives his Holy Spirit to you' (1 Thessalonians 4:8). And the Holy Spirit will gradually make us — along with God's providence and God's Holy Word — more and more like Jesus. He will gradually ripen in us Christ-like character, for 'the fruit of the Spirit is love, joy, peace, patience, kindness, goodness, faithfulness, gentleness, self-control' (Galatians 5:22,23).

IN CONCLUSION

So, the Bible teaches the need — the indispensable need — of the Holy Spirit's work in both regeneration and sanctification. The Holy Spirit of God both brings about our initial Christian birth and also facilitates our continuing Christ growth. He works salvation in us, and He enables us to work our salvation out! His sanctification of us is our glorification commenced. Our glorification will be this sanctification completed. So Christian, take heart! Say with the *Apostles' Creed* 'I believe in the Holy Spirit.' God has not finished with you yet! 'And I am sure that he who began a good work in you will bring it to completion at the day of Jesus Christ' (Philippians 1:6).

Our blest Redeemer, ere He breathed
His tender last farewell
A Guide, a Comforter, bequeathed
With us to dwell.

And every virtue we possess
And every victory won
And every thought of holiness
Are His alone.

Spirit of purity and grace

Our weakness pitying see

O make our hearts Thy dwelling place

And worthier Thee.

(Henrietta Auber 1773-1862)

QUESTIONS AND POINTS TO PONDER

1. Why are non-Christians desperately in need of the Holy Spirit?

2. Why are Christians still desperately in need of the Holy Spirit?

3. What does the Bible mean by 'regeneration'?

4. What does the Bible mean by 'sanctification'?

5. Can you testify to the gracious ministry of the Holy Spirit in your life? Can you thank God for the time when He made you alive to Christ? Looking back, can you thank God for His continued blessings and help since your initial conversion to Christ?

6. How is the Holy Spirit's presence made manifest in a person's life?

7. 'Be filled with the Spirit' (Ephesians 5:19).

CHAPTER ELEVEN

CHRISTIANS BELIEVE THAT THE JUSSTIFICATION OF THE SINNER BEFORE GOD IS BY FAITH ALONE

THE GOSPEL OF JUSTIFICATION

Perhaps the most systematic explanation of Christian salvation found in the Bible is contained in Paul's magisterial epistle to the Romans. The one overarching theme of Romans is 'Justification by Faith.' The *Shorter Catechism* asks the question 'What is justification?' and gives the matchless answer.

'Justification is an act of God's free grace, wherein He pardoneth all our sins and accepteth us as righteous in His sight, only for the righteousness of Christ imputed to us, and received by faith alone' (Q. 33).

The Christian gospel proclaims that guilty sinners may be declared 'not guilty' or acquitted and even declared completely righteous at God's bar of judgment. And they may be so because of God's saving grace in the Lord Jesus Christ. On Calvary's cross Christ died in the place of sinners. He bore the penalty they deserved — He served their sentence — so that the believing sinner might be exonerated. Furthermore, because of Calvary, God is able to credit the unrighteous sinner with Christ's perfect righteousness. One of the most profound verses in the whole of Scripture says that, at Calvary, 'For our sake he made him to be sin who knew no sin, so that in him we might become the righteousness of God' (2 Corinthians 5:21).

Calvary was therefore a saving transaction. Christ, the sinless one, took our sins, so that we, the sinful ones, might be accounted righteous before God — credited with Christ's perfect righteousness, attained by His sinless life, perfect obedience to God's law and the giving up of that life as an atoning sacrifice for others. A basic fundamental of Christian salvation is that we are not saved by our own righteousness — we actually have none — but by the perfect righteousness of Christ. A Christian is one who is 'found in him, not having a righteousness of my own, based on law, but that which is through faith in Christ, the righteousness from God that depends on faith' (Philippians 3:9). More briefly, a Christian is one who is 'justified by his blood' (Romans 5:9).

My hope is built on nothing less
Than Jesus' blood and righteousness
I dare not trust the sweetest frame
But wholly lean on Jesus' name.

When He shall come with trumpet sound
O may I then in Him be found!
Clothed in His righteousness alone
Faultless to stand before the throne.

On Christ the solid rock I stand
All other ground is sinking sand.

(Edward Mote 1797-1874)

THE MEANS OF JUSTIFICATION

The big question however is 'How are all the saving benefits of Christ received?' 'How may the blessings of Christ — the blessings of forgiveness, acceptance and justification — be made my own?' The answer of the Bible is 'By faith' — or more specifically, 'by faith in Jesus Christ. The *Shorter Catechism's* definition here is, once again, hard to beat.

'What is faith in Jesus Christ?'

'Faith in Jesus Christ is a saving grace, whereby we receive and rest upon Him alone for salvation, as He is offered to us in the gospel' (Q. 86).

The Bible describes the Christian's justification from various angles. It affirms that we are 'justified by his grace as a gift' (Romans 3:24). It affirms 'we are now justified by his blood' (Romans 5:9). It affirms 'It is God who justifies' (Romans 8:33) and it affirms 'that a man is justified by faith apart from works of the law' (Romans 3:28). These are all complementary rather than contradictory truths. They all show that justification is God's work, not the sinner's. They show that justification is solely due to the grace of God, in Christ, at Calvary. But how is this saving grace received? By faith. Faith is the channel — the receptacle — through which the blessings and benefits of salvation come to us. In affirming that the justification of the sinner before God is by faith alone, we are affirming that salvation is by divine grace, not human graft, by divine mercy, not human merit — that 'a man is not justified by works of the law but though faith in Jesus Christ, even we have believed in Christ Jesus, in order to be justified by faith in Christ, and not by works of the law, because by works of the law shall no one be justified' (Galatians 2:16). In Ephesians 2:8 and 9 Paul — who before His conversion worked zealously with a view of being right with God — explained and exclaimed the rock foundation of the Christian Faith in the words 'For by grace you have been saved through faith, and this is not your own doing, it is the gift of God, not because of works, lest any man should boast.'

FAITH ALONE: A BASIC, BASIC

'Faith alone' was the motto of our Protestant forefathers, when they protested against the human works righteousness promulgated by the Roman church as being contrary to the Bible. The Reformers proclaimed 'faith alone' as they wished to stress that salvation is gained by what Christ has done for us and not what we supposedly do for God. 'Faith alone' rules out all notions of human merit.

Bishop JC Ryle wrote the following helpful explanation of what it means to have saving faith in Christ:

'Saving faith is the *hand* of the soul. The sinner is like a drowning man at the point of sinking. He sees the Lord Jesus Christ holding out help to him. He *grasps* it and is saved. This is faith (Hebrews 6:18). Saving faith is the *eye* of the soul. The sinner is like the Israelites bitten by the fiery serpent in the wilderness, and at the point of death. The Lord Jesus Christ is offered to him as the brazen serpent, set up for his cure. He *looks* and is healed. This is faith (John 3:14). Saving faith is the *mouth* of the soul. The sinner is starving for want of food, and sick of a sore disease. The Lord Jesus is set before him as the bread of life, and the universal medicine. He receives it and is made well and strong. This is faith (John 6:35). Saving faith is the *foot* of the soul. The sinner is pursued by a deadly enemy and is in fear of being overtaken. The Lord Jesus is put before him as a strong tower, a hiding place and a refuge. He *runs* into it and is safe. This is faith (Proverbs 18:10)' (*Old Paths*, pp. 228 f.).

The justification of the sinner before God is therefore by faith alone. By faith we personally appropriate all the blessings of salvation gained for us by Christ. In the Bible, faith in Christ, trusting Christ and believing in Christ are synonymous. They amount to the same thing. Interestingly, one of the many synonyms for a Christian is . . . a believer. 'More than ever *believers* were added to the Lord' (Acts 5:14, author's emphasis). 'The word of God . . . is at work in you *believers*' (1 Thessalonians 2:13, author's emphasis). And the exhortation of the Christian gospel to sinners is '*Believe* in the Lord Jesus, *and you will be saved*' (Acts 16:31, author's emphasis).

Not saved are we by trying
From self can come no aid
Tis on the blood relying
Once for our ransom paid
Tis looking unto Jesus
The Holy One and just
Tis His great work that saves us
It is not try but trust.

No deeds of ours are needed
To make Christ's merit more
No frame of mind or feelings
Can add to His great store
Tis simply to receive Him
The Holy One and Just
Tis only to believe Him
It is not try but trust.

(E.G. Taylor 1830-1887)

Justification. It is a cardinal Christian doctrine. Christians are those who have been and are 'justified by faith.' The Bible teaches that the justification of the sinner before God is by faith alone. This is the distinguishing mark of biblical Christianity, foundational to authentic Christian experience and a continuing source of wonder, thanksgiving, and joy.

'We are accounted righteous before God only for the merit of our Lord and Saviour Jesus Christ by faith, and not for our own deservings. Wherefore, that we are justified by faith only is a most wholesome doctrine, and very full of comfort . . . ' (*39 Articles.* Chapter XI 'Of the Justification of Man').

QUESTIONS AND POINTS TO PONDER

1. Why does the Bible say that we are justified by faith, but elsewhere say we are justified by grace and elsewhere that we are justified by God? Is it contradicting itself?

2. How do non-Christian religions seek to be right with God? How do people with no religion at all hope that 'all will be OK in the end'?

3. Why is the biblical doctrine of justification 'a most wholesome doctrine, and very full of comfort'?

4. Task. Memorise the *Shorter Catechism's* definition of justification.

5. 'Justification is the mark of a standing or falling church' (Martin Luther). When was the last time your minister preached on this doctrine?

6. 'Therefore, since we are justified by faith, we have peace with God through our Lord Jesus Christ' (Romans 5:1).

CHAPTER TWELVE

CHRISTIANS BELIEVE THAT THE NEW BIRTH RESULTS IN AND IS MADE EVIDENT BY HOLINESS IN ONE'S LIFE AND GOOD WORKS CARRIED OUT

THE WONDER OF CONVERSION

In 2 Corinthians 5:17 the Apostle Paul exclaims, 'Therefore, if any one is in Christ, he is a new creation; the old has passed away, behold, the new has come.' Interestingly, the original Greek has no actual word for 'is' here. Paul is almost spontaneously blurting out here 'If anyone in Christ: new creation.' A Christian therefore is one who has been transformed by Christ and transformed eternally — just as Paul himself was never the same again after his life-changing encounter with the glorified Christ on the Damascus road. When we consider the absolutely radical change which a saving encounter with Christ brings, if a person professes to belong to Him, but continues on in their old ways and persists in a sinful manner of life, we have just cause to doubt the reality of their salvation. A profession of faith does not always signify the possession of true, saving faith.

FAITH WORKS!

We saw in a previous chapter that the Bible teaches that we are saved by faith alone, as we are saved by Christ alone — and that is the literal gospel truth. Yet the Bible is also adamant that faith works, that is, that the reality of our saving faith will be manifest towards others, as it is lived out in this fallen world. The word 'Christian' actually means 'Christ's one.' Christians are to reflect that they do indeed belong to Christ. Christians are called to reflect something of the One who proclaimed to be the 'light of the world' (John 8:12). The Saviour Himself exhorts His followers in all ages to 'Let your light so shine before men, that they may see your good works and give glory to your Father who is in heaven' (Matthew 5:16).

Saving faith is a work of the heart. As such, it cannot be seen. Saving faith however, whilst unseen, can yet be evidenced — evidenced in our lifestyle — our thoughts, words, deeds, appetites, ambitions, desires and even our dreams! In Ephesians 2:8,9 Paul states, 'By grace you have been saved . . . not because of works.' But then in the very next verse he continues 'For we are his workmanship, created in Christ Jesus for good works, which God prepared beforehand, that we should walk in them' (Ephesians 2:10).

Sinless perfection and total sanctification — as we intimated previously — is for the life to come, not the present life. Yet if our salvation is real, it will surely be evident by a degree of holiness of life. In 1 John 3:6 we read the searching verse 'No one who abides in him sins; no one who sins has either seen him or known him.' The verse does not teach sinless perfection, as the verb employed is a continuous one. John's first letter assumes that Christians will sin and have lapses — 'If we say we have no sin, we deceive ourselves, and the truth is not in us' (1 John 1:8). The sense of the verse is more like 'No one who abides in Him continues to sin.' It is saying that a habitually sinful lifestyle — as opposed to the occasional lapse through weakness — contrary to the will of God as revealed in the Bible is a lifestyle which casts aspersions on and even negates any profession of faith made with the lips. Our habitual words and deeds betray the condition of our heart. It is a case of a sound root producing good fruit. It is not the fruit itself which makes a tree alive, but a living and healthy tree will certainly bear good fruit. Jesus Himself said, 'every sound tree bears good fruit, but a bad tree bears evil fruit. A sound tree cannot bear evil fruit, nor can a bad tree bear good fruit. Every tree that does not bear good fruit is cut down and thrown into the fire. Thus you will know them by their fruits' (Matthew 7:17-20). Good works do not produce the new birth. But the new birth produces good works.

PAUL AND JAMES ARE ONE

Historically, Paul and James have been accused of contradicting each other. Critics suggest that Paul teaches justification by faith whereas James teaches justification by works. This thought is based on a misunderstanding. We can state categorically that the Holy Spirit who inspired the Bible never contradicts Himself.

Paul teaches how we may be justified before God Himself. James though is concerned with how we may be recognised as being justified before others. James is warning against an empty profession of faith. This is what James means when he states, 'You see that a man is justified by works and not be faith alone' (James 2:24). James is concerned with the evidence for justification. He concludes, 'For as the body apart from the spirit is dead, so faith apart from works is dead' (James 2:26). James is warning us against a dead faith and an empty profession. Like Paul, he is causing us to 'Examine yourselves, to see whether you are holding to your faith' (2 Corinthians 13:5). An old illustration goes like this: 'If you were arrested on suspicion of being a Christian, would there be enough evidence to convict you?' It is a searching question . . .

Good works do not produce the new birth. But the new birth produces good works. It is a searching question . . .

A WONDERFUL CHANGE

So the new birth results in a radical transformation in a person's heart and life. The new birth does not bestow an instant sinlessness and a perfect sanctification, but it does bring about a change, sometimes dramatic and drastic, but more usually a gradual one. There is no quick way to holiness, yet the new birth results in and is made evident by holiness and a desire for holiness — a God centred life. The new birth is also made evident by good works being carried out — the desire to please God as much as it is possible for a saved sinner to do. It has been well said that salvation is all of grace and works are all of gratitude. We have established that we are not saved by works, but we are saved for works. Seek therefore both to be what God would have you to be and do what God would have you do. Faith works! Bishop JC Ryle put it very well when he wrote: The Lord Jesus bids you 'occupy.'

By that He means that you are to be a 'doer' in your Christianity, and not merely a hearer and professor. He wants His servants not only to receive His wages, and eat His bread, and dwell in His house, and belong in His family, but also to do His work. You are to 'Let your light so shine before men that they may see your good works.' Have you faith? It must not be a dead faith; it must 'work by love.' Are you elect? You are elect unto 'obedience.' Are you redeemed? You are redeemed that you may be a 'peculiar people, zealous of good works.' Do you love Christ? Prove the reality of your love by keeping Christ's commandments. Oh reader, do not forget this charge to 'occupy.'

I would not work my soul to save
For that my Lord has done
But I would work like any slave
For love of God's dear Son.

Oh how I love Jesus

Because He first loved me.

(attributed to St. Patrick of Ireland)

QUESTIONS AND POINTS TO PONDER

1. If we are saved by the grace of God in Christ, does it really matter how we live?

2. 'Non-Christians work to be saved. Christians work because they are saved.' Discuss.

3. 'Salvation is all of grace. Works are all of gratitude.'

4. 'If you were arrested on suspicion of being a Christian, would there be enough evidence to find you guilty?'

CHAPTER THIRTEEN

CHRISTIANS BELIEVE THAT AT DEATH THE SPIRIT OF MAN DOES NOT CEASE TO EXIST OR BECOME UNCONSCIOUS

The late Bertrand Russell, a highly esteemed British philosopher, once allegedly said, 'When I die I rot.' A Christian would say 'He knows better now!', for his opinion was completely contrary to the Word of God, the Bible. And his opinion surely goes against what we all instinctively know: that this life is not the only life; there is a life beyond this short life. '(God) has put eternity into man's mind . . . ' (Ecclesiastes 3:11). The Bible teaches that at death the spirit or soul (the words are synonymous) of man does not cease to exist or become unconscious.

GOD'S SPECIAL CREATION

Scripture teaches that human beings are in a different category from the animal creation, for Scripture reveals that human beings were made by a direct act of God and that they are made in His own image. Because of this we all possess an immortal soul. Why? Because God made us so. We were not there when God created the first man and woman — Adam and Eve — but God has graciously revealed to us how He did this, so that we may know our origins. Genesis 2:7 describes how 'The LORD God formed man of dust from the ground, and breathed into his nostrils the breath of life, and man became a living being.' Our immortal souls originate from this divine breathing into us of the 'breath of life.' We will live forever! We will not however all live forever in the same place, for the Bible distinguishes between the saved and the lost, the condemned and the justified and heaven and hell. The difference between the two is saving faith in the Lord Jesus Christ.

THE DYING THIEF: A CASE STUDY

When Christ died at Calvary, two criminals were also crucified with Him 'one on either side, and Jesus between them' (John 19:18). One of these criminals was given the grace to turn to Jesus for mercy. He acknowledged both his own guilt and Jesus' guiltlessness, and said 'Jesus, remember me when you come into your kingdom' (Luke 23:42). Jesus replied to him 'Truly, I say to you, today you will be with me in Paradise' (Luke 23:43).

All outward appearances would suggest that the body of that anonymous criminal was taken down from the cross that afternoon and thrown into a common grave and began the process of decomposition. That surely was the case. Yet that was not the full story! Why? Because he had an immortal soul, and Christ had bestowed salvation upon him. He did not cease to exist or become unconscious. He went from being a condemned criminal to becoming a redeemed sinner to being a glorified saint. He moved from pain to Paradise! And it is the same and will be the same with every Christian, saved by grace. We too will likewise enjoy the same Paradise as that criminal, when our physical bodies are buried in the ground. We too will bask in the nearer presence of the Saviour — 'With me in Paradise.' We do not cease to exist or become unconscious at death. Job asked the question 'If a man die, shall he live again?' (Job 14:14). The answer of the New Testament is a resounding 'Yes!' because, for the Christian, death is the porter which ushers us into the nearer presence of God and we will be acutely conscious that this is so.

This life therefore is not the only life. The Apostle Paul could say 'For to me to live is Christ, and to die is gain' (Philippians 1:21) and 'My desire is to

depart and be with Christ, for that is far better' (Philippians 1:23). He expressed
the same sentiments when he said, 'we would rather be away from the body
and at home with the Lord' (2 Corinthians 5:8). Heaven is currently populated
with 'the spirits of just men made perfect' (Hebrews 12:23) enjoying the presence of the Saviour in a fuller, richer way than they ever did here on earth
— 'More happy, but not more secure, the glorified spirits in heaven' (Toplady).

THE REALITY OF THE AFTERLIFE

If we deny that there is a conscious life after the present life, and that —
a la Bertrand Russell — 'when we die we rot', we are audaciously suggesting
that we are wiser than the Lord Jesus Christ, the very Son of God. He once
told of two men — a rich man and a poor man named Lazarus. The Saviour
relayed how both men died. The death of them was not the end of them,
however. 'The poor man died and was carried by the angels to Abraham's
bosom' (Luke 16:22), He said. Abraham is described three times in Scripture
as 'the friend of God' (James 2:23, Isaiah 41:8, and 2 Chronicles 20:7). So, the
expression 'Abraham's bosom' means that after death, Lazarus went into the
bliss and nearer presence of God. The rich man also 'died and was buried.' But
sadly, he went to 'Hades' and is described as 'being in torment' there (Luke
16:23). He was most definitely conscious, for he cried out 'I am in anguish in
this flame' (Luke 16:24). This shows that both heaven and hell are real places,
and that their inhabitants will be acutely conscious that they are there in one
of them. The rich man went to hell because he was smug and self-sufficient
— he had no love for God or others. He saw no need for saving grace. The
name 'Lazarus' however means 'help.' Perhaps Lazarus's poverty enabled him
to realise his dependence on God, and cry to Him for mercy. In the light of
eternity, the poor man was rich, and the rich man was poor . . .

To conclude therefore, we state that, when a believer dies, their conscious
soul goes straight to heaven, awaiting, in God's time, the final resurrection

— being reunited to their body, albeit now a glorified body, free from sickness, weakness, sorrow, sin, and death. 'For we know that if the earthly tent we live in is destroyed, we have a building from God, a house not made with hands, eternal in the heavens' (2 Corinthians 5:1). 'For while we are still in this tent, we sigh with anxiety; not that we would be unclothed, but that we would be further clothed, so that what is mortal may be swallowed up by life' (2 Corinthians 5:4).

Christians thus believe that at death the spirit of man does not cease to exist or become unconscious. We all possess an immortal soul. The question is not whether we will live eternally, but where exactly we will spend eternity. The gospel of Christ alone reveals the secret of a happy life, a happy death, and a happy eternity.

'The bodies of men, after death, return to dust, and see corruption: but their souls, which neither die nor sleep, having an immortal subsistence, immediately return to God who gave them; the souls of the righteous, being then made perfect in holiness, are received into the highest heavens, where they behold the face of God, in light and glory, waiting for the full redemption of their bodies. And the souls of the wicked are cast into hell, where they remain in torments and utter darkness, reserved to the judgment of the great day. Beside these two places, for souls separated from their bodies, the Scripture acknowledgeth none' (*Westminster Confession of Faith*, Chapter 32, 'Of the State of Men after Death').

Where will you spend Eternity?
This question comes to you and men
Tell me, what shall your answer be?
Where will you spend Eternity?

Many are choosing Christ today
Turning from all their sin away

Heaven shall their blessed portion be
Where will you spend Eternity?

Leaving the straight and narrow way
Going the downward road today
Sad will their final ending be –
Lost throughout all Eternity!

Turn and believe this very hour
Trust in the Saviour's grace and power
Then shall your joyous answer be
Saved throughout all Eternity!
(Elisha Albright Hoffman 1839-1929)

QUESTIONS AND POINTS TO PONDER

1. Why do Christians believe that this life is not the only life? List some biblical evidences for life after death.

2. How should a belief in life after death affect our life in the present world?

3. 'There is great gain in godliness with contentment; for we brought nothing into the world, and we cannot take anything out of the world; but if we have food and clothing, with these we shall be content' (1 Timothy 6:6-8).

4. 'The souls of believers are at their death made perfect in holiness, and do immediately pass into glory and their bodies, being still united to Christ, do rest in their graves till the resurrection' (*Shorter Catechism*).

CHAPTER FOURTEEN

CHRISTIANS BELIEVE THAT THE DEAD WILL BE RAISED EITHER TO LIFE OR TO CONDEMNATION AND BOTH THE BLESSING OF THE RIGHTEOUS AND THE PUNISHMENT OF THE UNRIGHTEOUS WILL BE ALIKE ETERNAL

LIVING IN THE FUTURE TENSE

For the Christian, the best is yet to be. History, according to the Bible, has a goal. That goal is the Second Coming of the Lord Jesus Christ in power and great glory. And when Christ comes again at the end of the age, all His people — whether dead or alive — will be raised to immortality. Their souls will be reunited with their bodies, and those bodies will be raised to a new and glorious sphere of existence. Their redemption will then be complete. They will be redeemed in both body and soul and fit to serve the Lord on a redeemed earth — 'a new heavens and a new earth' (2 Peter 3:13) and will do so with joy and satisfaction for all eternity.

There is therefore a vital, future facet to the Christian Faith. We currently live in the 'in-between times' — we live, paradoxically, in both the 'arrived' and 'not yet.' We are saved, we are being saved and we will yet be saved. 'But our commonwealth is in heaven, and from it we await a Savior, the Lord Jesus Christ, who will change our lowly body to be like his glorious body, by the power which enables him even to subject all things to himself' (Philippians 3:20,21).

THIS PRESENT TIME

Life in the body at the moment is subject to all the ailments of this fallen world — pain, illness, physical and mental handicap, and ultimately — unless Christ comes before we die — death. But Christians have hope — a confident expectation and anticipation based on the promises of God. Our full and final salvation awaits us, but it is more than certain; 'we wait for adoption as sons, the redemption of our bodies' (Romans 8:23). Truly, 'the sufferings of this present time are not worth comparing with the glory that is to be revealed to us' (Romans 8:18). Suffering is for the 'now.' But in the 'then', God 'will wipe away every tear from their eyes, and death shall be no more, neither shall there be mourning nor crying nor pain any more, for the former things have passed away' (Revelation 21:4). The Christian's future is therefore as bright as the promises of God. We shall yet be raised to eternal life and eternal blessing. Paradise lost will be Paradise restored. 'For the trumpet will sound, and the dead will be raised imperishable, and we shall be changed. For this perishable nature must put on the imperishable, and this mortal nature must put on immortality' (1 Corinthians 15:52,53).

'At the resurrection, believers being raised up in glory, shall be openly acknowledged and acquitted in the day of judgment and made perfectly blessed in the full enjoying of God to all eternity' (*Shorter Catechism*, Q. 36).

But wherein lies the future perfect blessedness promised to the Christian? Surely it is this: 'and so we shall always be with the Lord' (1 Thessalonians 4:17). We shall be with our blessed Saviour for ever and ever and ever!

THE OTHER SIDE OF THE COIN

If the Christian's prospects could not be better, the Bible teaches that the non-Christian's prospects could not be worse. Whilst the Christian — when Christ returns — will be raised to eternal bliss, the non-Christian will be raised to eternal condemnation. The Bible is very black and white. 'He who has the Son has life; he who has not the Son of God has not life' (1 John 5:12).

The torment of the non-Christian at Christ's Second Coming and its aftermath is beyond description and imagination. Paul foretells the time when 'the Lord Jesus Christ is revealed from heaven with his mighty angels in flaming fire, inflicting vengeance upon those who do not know God and upon those who do not obey the gospel of our Lord Jesus Christ' (2 Thessalonians 1:7,8). There are those who teach that hell is not eternal. They preach 'annihilation.' Such thought is a wishful thinking at odds with Scripture. Second Thessalonians 1:9 and 10 tells us that all non-believers 'shall suffer the punishment of eternal destruction and exclusion from the presence of the Lord and from the glory of his might, when he comes on that day to be glorified in his saints, and to be marvelled at in all who have believed . . .'

There is an eternal hell to avoid. It is this which gives the gospel its urgency and imperative. Now is the time to get right with God. Now is that time to believe in the Lord Jesus — to cling to the cross — and be eternally saved from eternal hell. 'Behold, now is the acceptable time; behold, now is the day of salvation' (2 Corinthians 6:2).

A holy God must punish sin. Christ took the punishment for the believer's sin on Calvary to deliver the believer from that punishment. Therefore, if we do not believe in Him, we have no Saviour. We have 'no hope and [are] without God in the world' (Ephesians 2:12). Christ is the only Substitute qualified to take the sinner's place. So, if we do not believe in Jesus, and avail ourselves of His saving work, we will pay the penalty for our sins ourselves — eternally, in hell, 'the second death, the lake of fire' (Revelation 20:14).

The Bible therefore teaches most clearly that, when Christ comes again, at the Last Judgment, the dead will be raised either to life or to condemnation, and both the blessing of the righteous and the punishment of the unrighteous will alike be eternal. In summary: 'He who believes in the Son has eternal life; he who does not obey the Son shall not see life, but the wrath of God rests upon him' (John 3:36).

Day of judgement! Day of wonders
Hark! The trumpet's awful sound
Louder than a thousand thunders
Shakes the vast creation round
How the summons
Will the sinner's heart confound!

See the Judge, our nature wearing
Clothed in majesty divine
Ye who long for His appearing
Then shall say 'This God is mine'
Gracious Saviour
Own me in that day for Thine.

At His call the dead awaken
Rise to life from earth and sea
All the powers of nature shaken
By His look, prepare to flee
Careless sinner
What will then become of thee?

But to those who have confessed
Loved and served the Lord below

He will say 'Come near, ye blessed
See the kingdom I bestow
You for ever
Shall my love and glory know.

(John Newton 1725-1807)

QUESTIONS AND POINTS TO PONDER

1. 'Hope' is a technical, Christian word. Christians have 'hope.' How does Christian hope differ from a worldly 'hope so'?

2. Whilst grateful for present blessings, for the Christian, the best is yet to be. In what way is this so?

3. Is it true to describe a Christian as both saved and not yet saved?

4. How would you respond to those who say that hell is not eternal?

5. William Booth, the founder of the Salvation Army once allegedly said 'Every evangelist should have a short visit to hell.' Why do you think he said that?

Soli Deo Gloria

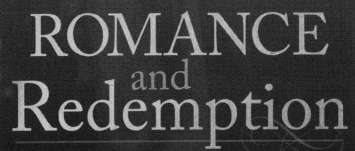

ROMANCE
and
Redemption

Enjoy the Book of Ruth

Timothy Cross,
BA (Hons), BD (Hons), Th.D., Litt.D

The book of Ruth is a moving story of romance and redemption. It begins tragically yet ends wonderfully.

Why? Because the God of the Bible 'is able to do far more abundantly than all that we ask or think' (Ephesians 3:20b).

In the book of Ruth we glimpse the wonderful providence of God at work. The book proves the truth of Romans 8:28 that 'in everything God works for good with those who love him, who are called according to his purpose.'

The book of Ruth is a story of romance—a romance between Ruth and Boaz—and also a story of redemption. Ruth, a nobody, became a somebody, eventually marrying into the Messianic line.

How? By the amazing grace of God. And it is the same today!

By nature we are sinners—helpless and hopeless. But by the grace of God in Christ, our sins are forgiven, and we become the adopted children of God and heirs of eternal blessedness—heirs of the very kingdom of heaven. These and others are some of the encouraging lessons we glean in the book of Ruth.

Come then and be blessed by this lovely portion of the Word of God and enjoy the book of Ruth!

For more information about

Timothy Cross
and
What Christians Have Always Believed
please visit:

www.TimothyJCross.org

For more information about
AMBASSADOR INTERNATIONAL
please visit:

Printed in Great Britain
by Amazon

56053521R00054